Easy Readin'

"Miscellaneous Titles"

authorHOUSE®

AuthorHouse™
1663 Liberty Drive, Suite 200
Bloomington, IN 47403
www.authorhouse.com
Phone: 1-800-839-8640

First published by AuthorHouse 2/5/2009

ISBN: 978-1-4389-3967-4 (sc)

Printed in the United States of America
Bloomington, Indiana

This book is printed on acid-free paper.

"Table of Contents"

"Follow Affection"

Follow affection, where ever you go

adjust to life's turns, experience and grow

despair can destroy and I feel you will find

life is more pleasant, if you're considered and kind

stepping on toes, to advance your own cause

can come back to haunt you, like unspoken laws

life has decisions, choice and convictions

it's imbedded within us to know right from wrong

live on forever, or is life a fleeting matter

whatever the question, the answer remains

possibilities are unlimited

and so are your sources

use judgment and conscience

as you plot your own courses

if you're sincere and your focus is in the right direction

your frustrations are technical and are not failure

though you stumble and fall

and feel you're unable

you have a set meaning

and cards on the table

adjust as necessary to fulfill your meaning

attune to your feelings; your sixth sense is keen

Though you set out to proceed with the best of intention

you may discover improvement

or a change in your plan

you may find there is virtue in a change of direction

and you shouldn't hurt anything, if you follow affection

"I'm addicted to money" - (congressional version)

I'm addicted to money and I just want to spend it

I'd like to cut down but it's not in my blood

I have programs and consultants, studies and staffs

I know I'll need more, so I want you to send it

Don't be concerned about your own education

worry not about your savings or even your family

You won't need a future or even a career

with me in the government, you have nothing to fear

I'm going to set up a program,

in fact I'll have several for just about everything

efficiency beyond belief, just wait you'll see

Just a little more time and money

and I'll put this all into action

it'll be better than before

it'll be to your satisfaction

the government will guarantee

So don't question; just send me more money

The tip of the iceberg is beginning to show

I know I have things that need doing

Don't worry; I'll take care of it,

you don't even need to know

These must be withdrawals, this feeling

that's better now; I feel more government waste coming on

don't wait any longer, I am the money monger

post-haste now, 'cause it's already gone

Look at this now, another program

this one will go smoother than the last program went

it'll cost more at first but then it'll get better

and anyway, the money's already spent

So I'm certain I'll beat this addiction

I'll give it a government guarantee

and anyway, the tax dollars will pay for it

so there's nothing to loose, in fact, it's free

so just a few more dollars

and my addiction will be almost over

I'll start my treatment just as soon as you send it

there's a government guarantee

so your money is safe

even if I don't recover

I promise, I won't spend it

"The Animal Kingdom"

The animal kingdom, what a phenomenal thing

All it encounters and all that it is

All breeds and all species, all models and makes

Just imagine, and then think, what imagination it takes

So many of them, and each a world of their own

Their life styles and habitats

Their instincts and habits

So cute when they're little and big when they're grown

But then, not all get that big

Some stay pretty small

I guess they're really all sizes

Well, not really all

and what about the dinosaurs

I guess they got pretty big

but it's been quite a while

I guess they're known as animals

Do they fit in that class

But now they're extinct, a thing of the past

But they are well remembered

well studied, and respected

never forgotten, and not really neglected

But back to the future, or the present I guess

the modern animal kingdom, the ones now on hand

All these species and kinds

well now that's a thought; can you tell me this

has anyone ever checked, I wonder,

do animals have minds

No, probably not, but what do I know

I could only make a guess, or ask somebody else

But I know they have brains and bones, and eyes and ears,

a body, a head, a mouth and a nose,

a stomach I guess, and basically everything else

At least most of them do, but then again there are so many

What about a snake, they have no arms

they're animals aren't they

I guess they must be, what else could they be

I just don't know, I sure can't say

But back to lions and tigers and bears

and dogs and my cats and birds of the air

Well, are birds in the animal kingdom

Aw, who cares, I can't say

they sure can fly better than me

they have their own way

They make me look kinda simple

or earthbound at least

sometimes just one or two, sometimes several,

sometimes a flock o' geese

Count them all, look at their formation; where are they going

I guess south in the winter and then it's back north

boy, what a kingdom these animal things

What a way of life

or again come to think

How many ways of life

Anyway, it's sure more than I can figure

But I can say that lots of times

And then still there are wolves and rabbits and gophers & fish

Squirrels & ferrets & cougars

Chimpanzees, gorillas, bison and antelope,

wildebeests, elk and the old mountain goat

I'd like to have some of all or at least some of each

but again, as usual, it's really only a wish

But I would like to have a couple of elephants and cougars

a dog and some dolphins and a couple of whales

to protect me, keep me company and make me feel strong

give me rides, food for thought and also be a back up

just in case all my memory fails

So this is a dream world I've slipped into

But I can't say that it's really so wrong

Anyway, back to reality

Just as good in its own way

Has its own appeal

and it gives a good sign

and it's also good to know

that the kingdom of animals is really quite real

So again, there's so many; can't have 'em all

some are too big, giraffes are too tall

but sometimes you can have some of 'em

depends on what you can get

see how it goes, and see what you do

and whatever, remember,

take care of yourself

and be good to your pets

"The Answer Man"

The answer man doesn't exist

Why do I say that?

well, that's a good question

Or what if he does, and I'm just blatantly wrong?

Well, that's a possibility I guess I should consider

But I believe he does not and I couldn't resist

But still then, why do I say it

Why raise the subject anyway

Whoever said that there was an answer man

and what makes me so certain that there's not

I believe that there are many questions

in fact I'm certain there are some

and I know that there are many people

but questions go unanswered; does that mean that we're dumb

I think not necessarily

but as always, I really don't know

if the answer man was here, he'd tell us

but then we wouldn't have these problems would we

so who would be the answer man

and would he tell you and me

what we really want to know

what we really need to know

or would he just keep the answers to himself

and leave us in doubt

so still I believe, that there are these questions

there must be answers, but where can you find them

I think there's one source, and yes, only one

and that doesn't mean that you can necessarily find out

but be leery of fraudulent, counterfeit answer men

or women who would have you believe

that they have the answers and that they're the only source

you could be easily mislead, and waste a lot of life

not knowing all along where you went wrong

then you'll end up with even more questions

and needing more answers of course

but what about that one source

does one really exist

I really can't say for sure

but I hope that there is

so where or what or who could it be

where would you go, and where do you start

like I said before I don't know for sure

but I hope there's a God, and I guess try your heart

"All"

Well I suppose if I can,
I'll get going once again
It appears I've reached a stall
Once I find my direction, I'll be on my way
right now, my back's against the wall
Can't say for certain where to start
or where I'll be going
does it matter anyway?
I'm sure I'll get somewhere, sooner or later
but probably not today
I don't have a clue, but I'm sure there's a key
beat my head against the wall
just keep trying, 'cause that's all I can do
though I thought I'd tried it all

"Little Babies"

Little bitty babies; I mean itty, bitty

Little bitty small ones; brand new

It's good they're alive, let's help them survive

They're innocent and honest and cuter than you

They have a clean slate and they're in their own state

their eyes and their conscience are clear

Observe their surroundings; use your experience,

have insight and protect them from what they might fear

They look like good people, they soon will grow up

they're going to need a good friend

You're a big person; show them your strength,

be kind and give them a hand

The world we live in is bigger than us,

we have to accept limitations

Now think of the small ones; consider their future

and then consider the future generations

We seem to have found ourselves in somewhat of a mess

I'm not really sure where it started

But life will improve and get better with time

if we're sincere and honest and good hearted

Now call me a fool; and think that I'm silly,

I can't really argue right now

But if you knew me very well,

I'm sure you could tell

I make sense in the long run somehow

"Bang the drum slowly"

Bang the drum slowly and be not proud
to me you're obnoxious, annoying and loud
It's there in your face, it appears in your eyes
you seem to think you're something
you suppose that you're wise
When honest, true people,
real and sincere
exist in reality
not fainting in fear
unassuming
Then so many like you
who never have known
the depth of other people
and convictions they own
Yet you insist that you're special
attention should be paid to you
You offer only annoyance
you've nothing to do
You don't comprehend what you're missing,
what's meaningful and true
You can't find the meaning
in what others do
People come and people go
and other lives they affect
Existence has meaning
you wouldn't understand
When all the time you should have listened
you talked loud instead
You have this complex

it's there in your head

You still think that you're something

and you'll find out too late

when you've wasted your time and others

then you meet with fate

You know not what to say

or even to think

suddenly a loss for words

your mind is on the blink

You're better off dead, and you discover with regret

life and death now is real and only one can save you

What do you offer

where's your noise and wisdom now

Can you plead ignorance

escape reality somehow

Eventually you'll know

The choice is not yours

When your life on Earth comes to an end

You'll know this for sure

A friend of mine, Otis Swet died February 4 1993. This poem was written on that day and he is remembered in it. Otis was a Pearl Harbor Survivor and retired from Puget Sound Naval Shipyard at age 62. Otis was 72 at the time of his death and had been a friend of mine for about 3 years. Otis was good natured, and pleasant to be around. I attended a Memorial for Otis at the local VFW. In Bremerton, WA

"Teddy Bears & Elephants"

Teddy bears and elephants
 and old Oliver Goose
some snowballs, mountaintops
 and one bull moose
Birds all alone,
 flying along in a flock
a small-town firehouse,
and a park, and a clock
Old Mother Nature and old Father Time
What do they all have in common
Where do their paths all meet
or does it even matter
Is this something that we should know
or even could know
No; it's just imagination, fascination
Something to think about, or wonder
Maybe food for thought, or just
some interesting things in a silly little rhyme
But this is nothing too important
so I wouldn't strain my brain
But if you ever come to Washington,
you're sure to enjoy the rain
More in some parts than in others
I've mainly seen the northwest
But Washington's a pretty big state
and I'm sure all parts are best
But as in all things, I guess it depends, on what you're looking for
and as for the rain, I guess you would tend to enjoy it more
if you like the rain of course

And if it looks like a duck and swims like a duck

and walks and quacks like a duck

then it's probably a duck

and that's a pretty safe bet

and what do you think when you look at a horse

I just mention the horse because they're so impressive

and so nice to look at

so many things are

Beauty in all faces, and almost all places

Only evil is what is so wrong

Evil is bad news and ugly to the bone

So what's really important and what does it matter

How much do you know and how much do I not

Where will the world go and how will we get there

Will we figure it out as we go along

"Bearings Straight"

Keep your bearings straight, wherever you go

Focus your mind and attention

Memorize everything that happens

Just kidding; use your mind and use what you know

Observe experience; evaluate results

Find out how it's done and what happens

Keep consequences in mind as you prepare a plan of action

Use judgment in achieving your goal

Keep your sights set, keep your mind on your objective

but then your brain and your eyes get so tired

so remember the important things

write them down if you have to

at least enough so you won't get fired

But life is not all a joke

and I don't say this lightly

and certainly some things are not funny

Sometimes life's harder than you can believe

and it's hard to believe that you have to depend on money

So as I said as I started, use good judgment

and consider consequences in setting your goal

But above all, be good and don't loose it

and at all cost, don't sell your soul

"What would be Bliss?"

What would life be if it wasn't like this
never a problem, no complications
Everything's beautiful, everything's easy
total tranquility, serenity and bliss
Where would we go, what would we do
we wouldn't know what to think
where is the glory in manning a ship
that could not even possibly sink
But it would be nice, it should be good
Maybe I'd like to try it
I might want this, I might want that
and I wouldn't even have to go out and buy it
Everything's provided, it's all yours
it's all right there for you
This life contains no challenge, nothing goes wrong
so then what would we do
It's a funny question, a funny thought,
what is reality?
In the present world it's so many things
more than we ever see or do
Anyway, it's not going to happen
this change will not occur
Reality exists, it won't change, it won't budge
and its course you can not stir
so I'll be content to do my best
at least, I hope I will
I'd rather be content than do my best
But if I can do them both, better still

"If"

If you can find God
It doesn't matter how old you are

"These Days"

It seems like every time I turn around

another day has passed

So now the future

That I used to plan for and think about

has gotten here at last

are things what I had looked forward to and expected?

is this what I wanted?

It's really hard to say

I know that every time I wake up again

it's only a few more hours

and there's another day

It used to be, I couldn't wait for tomorrow

And nowadays it seems

that although it never actually comes

it's always in my face

Where do I find myself when it really does arrive

Will I have done all I wanted to

Will I have achieved great things

Will I be in my place

probably no

It will be just another step

in the treadmill race

But all in all

What I don't understand

or what I haven't done

doesn't have to hold me back

or leave me discouraged

and I know that sooner or later, the future

that I've been looking for

will have gotten here at last

How will I deal with it then

and what will I think

of what I've done so far

I'll figure it out as I go along

and I'll know when I get there

tomorrow

when today becomes the past

"A Little Bit"

A little bit of life, that's what it is
a little bit of life, it's unbelievable
a little bit of life, that's what you've got
a little bit of life, it's inconceivable
a little here, a little there
it really is phenomenal
there's another little bit of life
I tell you it's incredible
there's a couple little bits of life
there's actually a lot
life itself, and a certain amount of sanity
life in its purest form
life void of ego, greed and
some other undesirable ingredients
and basically, no real vanity
it's a little bit of life, and a certain amount of sanity
that's what there is and that's what you can get
it's a little bit of life
in fact, it's an animal
it's a little bit of life
and sometimes, it's a pet

"Don't let me go"

Don't let me go

don't let me go

just don't let me go

thank you

I'm writing this on 1 October 1993 as I was typing other material. I'm typing and watching NBC's Nightline. Tonight's edition is about Mary Fischer, the relatively well known woman who became HIV positive through marriage and has lost her husband to the virus. She is the woman who spoke at the 1992 republican convention. As she was speaking at a school or some community event about the HIV virus, she went out into the audience to greet, shake hands with and hug some of the audience members. As she came by a young girl, I believe about 12 years old, the young girl hugged her and told her that she also had the virus, and the two of them just hugged and I could just imagine (which I obviously couldn't comprehend) the feeling of the young girl who just wanted to be held. This is dedicated to them and to anyone else who might appreciate it. I was crying as I watched the show and typed the above.

"Books & Pages"

Books and Pages, from so many ages

What do they all mean?

Where do they all lead?

Some speak volumes, just waiting to be seen

They're yours if you want them

If you know how to read

"Born to Be"

Looking around sometimes

so what's left to be said

some thinking out loud and some things that I've read

some over here, more over there

all different places, always somewhere

What's it about

or what does it matter

who wants to know, and how can they see

there's only one meaning

and they come out the same

it always comes back

to what we're born to be

Life's short in its own way, but then there's the long run

not everything's that hard, but nothing's that easy

things come and go, and things remain the same

always doing something, but nothing gets done

so it's around the corner and up the block

it's up to me now and it's around the clock

does it make any difference, and what is the matter

is there another way out, am I the only one

so what happens now, and how can we see

I've done that before, and it's not that much fun

I guess this goes here, and here we go again

and then it comes back to what we were born to be

"Buried Treasure"

The buried treasure, is not easy to find

it lay stealth and secure

safe from mankind

how many journeys

over seas

through the skies

how many searches

what truths and what lies

the location of the treasure

some would think, underground

but the treasure itself

is yet to be found

as life's phenomena

are studied and discovered

the secret of the treasure

has not been uncovered

men search and they seek

they struggle and wonder why

where will it be found, this treasure

can it be seen with the eye

look inside, I recommend

a chance that you'll find

the treasure you seek

exists in your mind

"Cards and Decisions"

It's not necessarily what you want
but it may well be what you get
keep in your mind, that life deals the cards
but remember, you place the bet
you can cut, shuffle, fold or stand pat
keep alert to what's around you
know where you're at
life's filled with crossroads, choices and decisions
your actions and decisions determine what you will be
not everything's that hard; but nothing's that easy
many things are costly, but some things are free
your choices and decisions are influenced by what you want
what you get will influence your actions and results
you don't always have a choice
the decision is not always yours
but concentrate, keep focused
set your mind on the long run
life has compromise, losses and gains
I recommend the considered, methodical approach
good thought and good judgment, all things considered
improve your techniques as you go along
insight and information are out there, you have the resources
be thoughtful and thorough, you'll go only so wrong
don't make big mistakes, don't over-worry about small ones
get good advice, good opinion, let your mind do the work
avoid people that cheat you and make you uneasy
don't be taken in by an angle or a scam

your focus is on the future, and it's also today

growth is in experience, many things, many ways

figure it all out sooner or later, can't solve it all right now

but if our focus is in the right direction

we'll get where we're going somehow

"Help us"

Pray for me
and I'll pray for you
Help me if you can
and I'll see what I can do
Is it possible that we can
answer the call
help ourselves
help each other
Heaven help us all

"End Run"

Having given some thought my friend
I recommend
that your actions in life
be considered and ruled from the heart
I expect in the end
whether we like it or not
we'll gain an incredible awareness
of just what this life is
whether a little or whether a lot
whatever you think, the actions you take
will have their effect on others
a search of the mind
I think you will find
whether you look at it, or like it, or not
though it may seem odd
we are all bound by God
when the end comes
we're all bound
Till death do us part

"A Different Kind of Clause"

Sometimes a poem seems a funny way to write

but sometimes I find it quite neat

you can say different things and don't need a whole sentence

and sometimes you kinda can cheat

I guess it's what's referred to as poetic license

though I'm not certain the real definition

but if you can say what you mean and you mean what you say

then it helps to accomplish your mission

I'm not certain how to get a poetic license

I'm not certain where to apply

but if I find that I need one and can't work without it

then I'm certain I'll get one, at least I will try

so anyway, are these things sentences?

or are they even a clause?

"claws you say, my cats have good claws"

no, that's a different word altogether

get back to the poem, and remember as you read

poems are read with a pause

"they also have paws, I tell you they have four each"

no, you've done it again, they're two different things

between paws and pauses, and claws and clauses

they're different altogether indeed

"well then what's the difference, and how can you tell?

does it matter which one you use?"

yes, they have different meanings and are used in different places

and you spot them by how they are spelled

"so what's the purpose of a poem, does it say anything?"

not necessarily, at least not some of mine

with some I write something that I really mean

and with some I'm just spending my time

but back to sentences and clauses

and also the unspoken pause

"are they parts of our English and grammar?

and do I have to learn them myself?"

yes they are and you will have to know them

you must memorize all of the laws

well, you don't really have to memorize them

but you learn them and come to understand

as you learn they make sense and you remember as you go along

and before you know it, you'll know all the laws of the land

but at times you will stumble across something

and you're not really certain how it goes

but remember your English and grammar

you can understand poetry and prose

nobody can remember everything

and everyone sometimes gets stuck

but you don't really have to memorize these things

when you need to know something, you can just look it up

"It's a Game!"

It's only a game
and, no one wins anyway
He who finished last is also done
He who finished first, isn't finished anyway
It was only a game
And nobody won

"Cells of the Brain"

Alcohol kills brain cells; that's one reason not to drink

It takes its toll, and when you're not looking

you've lost your ability to think

It's not the dead brain cells that cause this condition

That's just my uneducated guess

I really don't know this, but I think there's something to it

of course I'm not a psychiatrician

The reason I say this is based on this reason

Though I'm not certain there is really any reason or rhyme

But it makes some sense

and I can say this with a little experience

and observations that I've made over periods of time

The dead brain cells either come back to life

or you can function without them

at least to some extent

though maybe you never reach 100 percent

but then who ever does, or then who does ever

according to some people - nobody - never

You never use your whole brain anyway

at least that's what they say

But it'd be better to have it available in case that you need it

Anyway, it's all above my head, or maybe as they say, it's all in my head

But it doesn't make much difference

The bottom line is the same

I can manage without alcohol

and my brain has returned to functioning

and I'm probably fortunate at this point that more cells are not dead

So that's why I say that it's not the dead brain cells

but the immediate influence of alcohol that suppresses the thought

But there's so much more to it, in case you're not familiar

I've learned a little about it, so I thought that I ought

Share this view and that one and a couple of others

Make a point if I can and maybe even some logic

The return of dead brain cells and a little of agility

But as I said there's so much more affected by this stuff

But it's amazing what comes back that you forgot you ever had

As I know there's not a whole lot that's much closer to magic

and the lifting of the curse that causes you to loose so much of your physical ability

But here's the big difference, so let's keep it simple

It's actually all the difference and all that matters anyway

For all you stand to loose, through your experience with alcohol

Believe me, it's great and there's nothing to gain

So for all that it's worth and whatever you think

if alcohol causes you problems, you may have one on your hands

But try as you may and fight as you can

Strong as you may be; a tough guy, a big man

There is one winning of this battle

and the rest of it is a loss

You'll find out the hard way

the extent of the cost

The winner is simple but not easy

and there's only one way to say it

If you personally want to beat alcohol

Take it Easy - Don't Drink

Take care

"Could Be"

Things could be better but they're not
I wouldn't necessarily say
that anything's that incredibly bad or terrible
at least not right now
I suppose it would be fair to say
that in general, in the long run
as far as I can tell, things are basically ok
Hard to say I guess, sometimes hard to tell
Having concluded that some things
just plain have no real or good solution
and that there's only so much that a person can do
I attempt what I can
and sometimes I throw my hands up
I try to figure things out
and sometimes, I figure "oh well"
What can I do, or will it do any good
should I try something else
will it make the desired difference
where do you go for guidance
on a matter like this
there're no references or books
where do you look
I guess, at this point anyway, I'll be satisfied
to accept that things could be better but they're not
but,
if I think of a way to improve them
I'll be certain to try, I always try anyway
so you can bet, I'll take a shot

"A World without Cats"

A world without cats
just where would we be?
no lions or tigers or cougars
no alley cats or strays
no mountain cats or toms
no more cats around the house
no more games of cat and mouse
no little baby cats, or their furry little moms
if suddenly they all were gone
just where would we end up
no cats to play with our loose ends of string
or to come in and wake us up
would we miss them at first, or maybe later on
does it matter, what's the answer?
there'd be no more leopard and no Bengal tiger
and of course, no more panther
could it end up a loss that we'd live to regret
no cats in the zoo, we wouldn't have them as pets
maybe everything would be more quiet
at least more than it is right now
There'd be no lion's roar to wake up the jungle
and of course, no cat's meow
what then do you think, if it all just died out
the whole kitten race
gone altogether
wiped off the map
no more cats to sit on your lap
no cat-food bowls or litter boxes
no furry little face

would it turn into a world with more mice and more rats

just where would we be, in a world without cats

"Make a Decision?"

I could make a decision
But then I might change my mind
Lots of things to be considered
Don't want to forget anything
Some variables that might change along the way
I probably know what's right
but there's more I have to find out
Take everything into consideration
and see what I get
Figure everything out in advance?
or maybe better yet
Figure it out as I go along
Deal with things as they come
If I take everything into consideration
use my head and good judgment
play my cards right, and accept good advice
and don't do anything stupid
I should go only so wrong

"Déjà Vu"

Deja Vu

it happened again

or did it

or was it just

Deja Vu

damn the bad luck

that was just it

I just missed it

or was it

or did I

or was it just

Deja Vu

that's happened to me before

or has it

I can't stand it

has it happened to you

how does it

what is it

or is it just

Deja Vu

"I'm a Trained Detective"

I'm a trained detective, I seek and I find

You cannot evade me, you've left something behind

I work alone, undercover

I'm never at rest

You'll try to deceive me

You'll find I'm the best

I know what you think and I know who you are

You attempt to escape, but don't get very far

Cover your trail, burn the bridge

do all of these things

then look over your shoulder

I'm up on the ridge

I won't force you to stop

I haven't stopped you yet

yet I observe; as deeper and deeper you get

You know why I follow

you know right from wrong

someday you'll come clean

you've known all along

you continue to deceive

and evade the real issue

you think that everything will be ok

if only you can get away

But you can't, accept it

play by the rules

You try trickery and flight

but I'm there every night

Who am I? Where did I come from?

How have I found you?

You think you know better than me

What makes me right?

and anyway

Who says that I make the rules?

It's like this, here's your answer

I'm only gonna tell you once

Turn around, look again

I'm your conscience, you fool

"Around"

Look at the world
turn it around
everything's falling
upside
down
can't see what you're doing
follow the sound
look at the world
and turn it around

"ABC" (the Alphabet)

By the time I learn the alphabet

I'll know almost everything and I'll be all set

When I make a decision, it'll be right you can bet

'cause I can learn anything, - it's all in the alphabet

There's always something you want

and there's usually something you need

and just think what you can do, if you know how to read

You can learn this and learn that and then learn something else

If you need to know more you can find out for yourself

In an atlas or encyclopedia you can find places you've never seen

You can find a lot more in the newspaper or maybe a magazine

you can find almost anything if you know where to look

if it happened or it exists you can find it in a book

"Is it in the Dictionary?"

If it's not in the dictionary, it doesn't exist

At least that's what they say; or something like that

Maybe that's not it, now I'm uncertain

I'm sure that's not a hundred percent right

It's probably inaccurate

I'm sure there's something more to it

But it's a quick, catchy phrase and I couldn't resist

The dictionary doesn't have everything; it couldn't

But it sure does have a lot

It doesn't have history, or much about science

But taking a look, you can sure learn a bunch

and might be surprised at all that it's got

Of course maybe you already know it all

then again; maybe not

I've read the whole dictionary six or eight times

not really, but it sounds good to say

and if I say it just right

and work my words well

I can play out a hunch and make it fit with my rhymes

But I do like to read through the dictionary

It's not something I do all the time

But sometimes I just page through

and look up the meanings

of some of the words that I often had wondered

Do you ever wonder, the exact definition of some words

that you basically know how to use

But if you had to define them, you'd be kinda stuck

and if your life counted on it, you'd be outa luck

But outa's probably not in the dictionary

and hopefully you won't end up with your life on a limb

over something so stupid, as the meaning of a word

'cause if you really had to know it, you could just look it up

So that's one of the things I do with my dictionary

but also I use it to make sure how to spell

but sometimes I don't feel like it, 'cause sometimes I'm lazy

so I just hope it's spelled right, and just figure "oh well"

But if it's important I'll make sure to check it

There's really no good reason why not

And also if it's really important, and it has to be right

Then I best look it up or I'll be on the spot

But it's ok, 'cause it's all in the dictionary

well, no, not really everything, but it has quite a bit

you can look up old words and new ones

words that you've heard or you've seen

double check to make sure that you know how they're spelled

and make sure that you know what they mean

So, now you might be starting to wonder

or maybe you started to wonder before

what about this poem, is everything spelled perfectly well

maybe you know, but if not, then how could you tell?

or is everything in here grammatically correct?

probably not

but if you had some references on English and grammar

and if you had a dictionary to use in your home

you could find out for sure, without much of a doubt

and I'd have to admit that you've probably got me

it's not a hundred percent correct

but I have an excuse and it's kinda hard to argue

'cause remember what you're reading

it's only a poem

"Please Don't"

He didn't see the sign that said
No Turn On Red
He proceeded without caution
And ended up dead
He's remembered by friends and family
Who wish he was still alive
By bumper stickers they place on their cars
that say
PLEASE
DON'T DRINK AND DRIVE

"Everybody at once"

Cut the federal deficit

Contain inflation

Maintain the national defense

Clean up white-collar crime and corruption

also government; and don't forget the streets

Streamline bureaucracy and improve the education system

Make government more effective and less of a burden

Be humble, fair and realistic

If you won't attempt this or it just can't be done

then tell me, why bother

and then answer this - "what's the use?"

Remember the rest of us couple hundred million saps

and while you're at it, put a stop to all fraud, waste and abuse

See if you can comprehend the value of a buck

Understand what you're doing before you commit

Comprehend reality before you set something into law

and before you run us all out of luck

These are among the things

people would like from the government

change, improvement and less intrusion

And the people should have a voice

Here's one thing we can do as a people

Take matters seriously

Learn about the circumstances

Use your resources

and use your head when you make a choice

Learn something about the people you're electing

find out who's who and what's what,

use your judgment

It's a big job, but someone can do it

at least I hope someone can

If no one can, then as a nation we're sunk

everybody at once, kids, women and men

Who has the answers

who has the keys

I hope that someone among us has a solution

and I do recommend that each one of us

make just this one contribution

Just one contribution?

Well, feel free to do more

but don't neglect this 'cause it counts

Though I don't have the answers

I can tell you one thing

"look now!" - "we're all in the same boat!"

but it won't get any better

so it just won't work

so it's just not worth it

if you just don't vote

take care

think before you vote

"Evil spirits, bad people and ghosts"

I don't believe in ghosts,
in fact I believe in God
all forms of evil may come and go
God remains eternal
Be they evil spirits or just terrible people
Try as they may they will not reach their goal
God is and always was
He is truly almighty
He alone can give life
He alone shares your soul

"The fall"

I know now that I will never fall in love
and now I know why
Because now I know that love will never fall for me
so there'll be no love for me to fall in
but if God is
and he will be fair to me
then I hope that, that is love
and I will know
for me, I believe there could be no other love
and I'm not certain about this

"The Promised Land"

America has found the Promised Land

In sex and rock & roll

It's easy to learn, at a very young age

You need look no further

To establish your goal

It's so easy my friend

And it's all that you could ever want

There is no talent required

And life is a breeze

There's money for nothing

chicks for free

and party till you drop

There are no harsh lessons

Or effort to learn

You'll have fame and fortune

And money to burn

No sacrifice required

And you don't have to read

Everything you need to know

Is easily available

It all can be found

Just by watching TV

"People - The only thing"

People, the only thing

not the only thing

not actually, not literally I guess

but in a way

interesting thought

what else is there?

of course there's plenty of other things

but what is there without people

other people

has to be people, for us to exist

elementary

but the thought means something

other things are plenty significant

I'm a big fan of animals myself

nature is obviously meaningful

people are what we are

that's what it is

people

this is where there is much meaning

find plenty of meaning in nature

find lots to appreciate in animals

people, other people are the center of our meaning

a hope that there's a God

or if you know personally, for certain

the definite existence of God

the reality that God is

that would be nice

good people, animals, some things in nature

and a hope that there's a God

pretty well make up the meaning of life

reason for living

speaking for myself

and frankly, without a hope in God

I'm not certain how much I'd be interested in anything else

over time - dealing with life as we know it

working with what we have

because that's what we have to work with

people are what our existence is about

and God if we can find him

everything will come from God

he is the soul source of existence

the existence of people must be his will

so actually God is all that there is

God and his will

so he must have created people

that's what we are

people

so if we can find God in our lives

that is probably what we should do

and accepting that he is

and accepting we are his will

then people are where

we should be able to find

some of what we're looking for

hopefully

but either way

this is where we live

our lives as we know it

"Fantasy?"

Retreating in fantasy?
maybe, maybe not
maybe it's fantasy
maybe it's thought

"More than a few"

More than a few, that's what I've got

That might be alright, but I think that it's not

If problems are many, and solutions are few

then I have a tendency to think that something's not right

problems all over the place, not a solution in sight

but right now I'm just saying this, everything's not all that bad

but sometimes it is and I can't see my way out

so what do you do when the problems out-weigh the solutions

you think you need help, and there're no contributions

can't solve it yourself, not this one at least

don't know where to start, so how will you ever overcome it

I don't know either; I've had problems like that

there must be a solution, but where is it at

can't find it at all, that darn solution

but the problem's right there, it won't go away

and that ominous feeling; the things here to stay

 this one needs a solution, better start looking

where to start on this one; here we go again

I didn't want this problem in the first place

so why is it mine

why not be someone else's problem

leave me out of it this time

but problems seem to have a way of finding their victim

they appear whether you want them or not, you don't have a choice

they seem to have no manners they don't even ask

they just land in your life and end up your task

you can't just dismiss them, or give them to somebody else

though some people try this; but it's not fair to other people

so what do you do when the problems start coming

and you know the solutions are way off in the distance

guess you have to take them as they come, use your ingenuity

ask for help and advice, in just this one instance

some people are all sorts of help, some aren't much at all

some will help more than expected, that's my kind of person

"if there were more people like you, we'd all be better off"

that's what I tell them

so thanks for the help, you made a big difference

I was getting nowhere and didn't know where to start

thanks again my friend, I sure won't forget this

and if I can help you, you know where to find me

so I'm sure there'll be more problems in the future

probably more than a few

but I think I can handle 'em,

I think I can, thanks to you

"America (kinder-gentler)"

A kinder, gentler America
it's there, in your soul
It's in who you are, and how you view
the world as a whole
Reality, the big picture
where you're from and how you go
what you find and do as you go along
what you believe, and what you know
Realization and recognition
of what's really wrong and what's right
and don't forget your resources
a thousand points of light
It's there and you can find it
it's all in who you are
a kinder, gentler American
a better place by far

"Food for Thought"

What is food for thought and where can you get it

I'm afraid to ask and not certain what I'll do

But then come to think of it, I guess if you consider

food for thought could be anything, it's all around you

people all have opinions, they all have their views

and there's all sorts of books, newspapers, all sorts of news

everyone has a mind, it allows them to think

it never rests, never sleeps, never a blink

It's a mystery to science, but let's keep it simple

your mind lets you think, not a mystery to me

feelings, emotions I guess they're all involved

does the mystery of the mind really have to be solved

Just think what you can do and think what you've done

life can be very serious, but some of it's fun

you can read and research, develop and discover

who knows what mystery you might uncover

but the mystery of the mind probably won't go away

be thankful you've got one and it's here to stay

you use it to think and it helps you understand

you probably use it in all that you do

you can commit things to memory and recall them at will

you can help solve some problems and better yet still

your mind is your own, no one else can have it

and just think about it, to you it was free

so there're lots of things in life that you should consider

choices, decisions, your friends and your job

get opinions, get advice, always use good judgment

and use your mind to determine just what you will be

many problems seem too much, unable to be solved

you're afraid to confront them and hesitate to get involved

think about it, use your best judgment and hope for the best

then be willing to adjust and improve as you go

consider your options, use your mind, put it to the test

put it to deep thought, think about it while you're sleeping

remember, your mind never rests

So, food for thought, well, I guess it's all around

depends on what you're looking for and what you make of it

different things are important to different people

your interests will change as you grow and get older

to whom is what important?

Do your best, don't carry the world on your shoulder

concentrate, focus, and remember - don't blink

but food for thought, who knows, I wonder

Well, you tell me

what do you think

"Hold a Candle"

Hold a candle, if you can
so that someone else can read
Take a back seat, on selected occasions
so that someone else may lead
Step up to the plate
if that's what is best
or step away
according to the circumstances
if that's what meets the test

"Unfinished Business"

Thankfully my friends, again we arrive

this year to Mother's Day

that certain day that we set aside

to say "thanks again" 'cause we're alive

once every three hundred and sixty five

in the lovely month of May

over time things will come and go

life itself may change

if we're lucky, we can get along ok

we hope that all will have a good day

we try our best and wish others well

but there's no guarantee that life will be easy

at least as far as I can tell

the game of life is never won

a mother's work is never done

we all have unfinished business

as we attempt to attain our goal

we take care of ourselves and help others when we can

we pray to God to save our soul

we hope that we will find some peace

at least when the day is done

as we consider our future

or reflect on our past

we wonder which things will change

and which will last

as life itself, goes left, right and upside-down

it's sometimes hard to find our aim

but be thankful my friend

one thing you can count on

Mom remains the same
so with a multitude of voices
and various tones
once a year, we tie up the phones
uncounted people with one thing to say
"Thanks Again, and Happy Mother's Day"

"Hardball" (My Multi-Talented Alter Ego)

When it's time to play hardball, I play like Dennis Eckersley

If it comes time to fight, like Roberto Duran

My arsenal is extensive, so don't call my bluff

You'll learn a quick lesson, you are not that tough

I am not dishonest and I don't cheat to win

I don't have to, I can beat you, you'll never begin

If I need a clutch hit, I'm like Tony Perez

Think you'll try me again

I'm like Julio Caesar Chavez

But when it comes down to life and death

and other serious matters

The sake of the nation and the people that I know

I will take no chances and I'll beat you without question

My tactics swift and sure, no stone left unturned

You think you'll endure, you will not, this is for certain

This time I'm serious, I'll play like Ross Perot

"Here goes"

Here goes life, here it is, there it goes

that was it, it's over now, it's over, it's over

well, it's not over yet, it's not over, it's still here

but that part's gone, that was it, it's done

what is this thing called life

where does it come from

where do we get it

where does it go, when it's over and done

I don't know

I suppose I could ask you

could you tell me; would you if you knew

I'd tell you if I knew, I'd give you a hint

but I don't know; now it's over, that was it

but it's not over, it's still here, here it is

it's bigger than I am, and I can't stop it

it keeps going,

it's been doing that for a long time

it's old and it's new

I think that's what it is

it's far in the past

and I don't know, but I'd bet

it's in the future too

but that's life, there it goes

I think that's what it is

anyway

there it is, and I'm not

I'm here for a while; a while or a time

a couple of sentences; some of 'em rhyme

sometimes I learn something; at least it's a thought

sometimes I'm thinking, sometimes I'm not

but that's life and that's me

and that's time

there goes

"Look Here"

Look in other people's faces
Look in the sky
And all other places
Look inside
And you might wonder why
This is life
We are here
We live
And we die

"If you ever grow up"

If you don't grow up, you may never grow up

May seem a silly thing to say; but, may be kinda true

Maybe you're responsible; on your way to maturing

Maybe this doesn't apply to you

You may already be grown, with a life of your own

who knows

well, I expect you do

I want to say "good for you" if you know what you're doing

Glad to see you're getting along

Of course, I don't even know you, I'm writing this blindly

it's inspired by some things I've observed

and some things I believe are contributing factors

to circumstances that seem to routinely go wrong

So, what do you care what I think

Of course, I can't answer that

Just like a lot of other things

a lot of answers, I don't have

Observations I've got

observations, some subjects for thought

and some things that need to be done

But don't we all

I would certainly think so

Along with a lot of other things, that's life

So don't miss out

and don't make lousy decisions

Learn what you're doing and learn how to do what you want

Getting discouraged is natural if you try very hard

So keep focused and just don't give up

But understand first

you won't have much of a chance

to get where you're going

if you never grow up

Take care

"Impossible Dream"

The impossible dream
the unreachable star
depends on what's possible
depends on where you are
sometimes you may well be able
able to reach or able to dream
something's may be easier
some harder than they seem
wherever you reach
whatever you attain
find meaning in life
not only in gain
ultimately, eventually
it should come back to this
may not always be easy or fun
may not always make sense, or have reason
may not seem right
and may sometimes seem odd
but I think that true meaning can be found
and likely, found only with God

"Justice"

There is no form
there is no color
there is no sound
and there is no smell
it's both big and small
it can be discovered
if viewed correctly, it's right
but how can you tell

"Once Upon a Time" (a place called home)

Once upon a time
In a place called home
Scattered remnants still exist in my mind
But, you don't know what you've got, till it's gone
And by then, it's really impossible to find
The shell breaks
The clock's already running
It's time for you to roam
And no my friend, you can't go back
Reminiscing in a poem

"Lines and Levels"

Lines and levels
tables and planes
weights and measures
money and scales
what's within and what's not
the range of a scope
blue skies and sunshine
trees and water
air and vegetation
a little bit of hope

"If the shoe fits, wear it" (how to treat your enemies)

You're not getting away and I'll tell you why

you've trapped yourself, and will now know defeat

I know what you think and I know what you try

you think that your plan is impressive, but guess what

it's your personal destruction, you've dug your own grave

my plan has you for the fool that you are

you think you've done something, you assume that you're clever

your existence is now over, comprehend - never

you're simple and you're selfish and I'm teaching you a lesson

you've got it all figured out, - try again

you think that you're smart, but you're dead in your heart

and for you it's too late for confession

you reach only one goal

and I'll not save your soul

you'll soon loose your mind

and guess what else you'll find

guess, guess, guess, guess, guess

you're lost, that was it

life for you is now over

in fact you never have lived

and love has never known you

you've wasted good air

but infinity will not be harmed

you're a pitiful helpless maggot

and you'll not be able to breath

you're simple and you're small

but guess what, that's not all

you'll never understand

you're surrounded and unarmed

"God Is"

Last night I thought I understood God

but now I've forgotten

damn it; I had it right there

It was as if I knew

It was a pretty good feeling

that was all I needed

Now I've forgotten, and I don't know where to look

I know God is there, but will I ever find him

I don't know, and I don't know what to say

but if God is, and he is as I thought

then I'll be glad and I hope he finds me

and if he does, then I believe that all the things

that I worry about and wonder

will somehow be ok

"God only knows"

There's a reason for everything
but some of 'em don't make any sense
now I'm searching for another line
and I suppose I have to make it rhyme
Ha! I did it
at least that's close enough
but does this make any sense
that's the important thing
and is yet to be determined
it already doesn't rhyme
but what sense does it make
or does it actually have to
and what, in this case, is the reason
could be a lot of things
maybe not
although there are a lot to be considered
I suppose some are more significant than others
or maybe more important
at least they seem to be
what's more important in life
or what, I guess, is less
some things in life seem to be a problem
sometimes they're just there
you can't always solve 'em
they don't always seem to make any sense
or even have a reason
but sometimes things come out ok
some things have a funny way of making sense
I guess they make sense in their own way

so what do you do

try, I guess

I really don't know

hope for better in the future

and help when you can

remember mom and dad

and whether or not you become one your self

do what you can to help others

so what's the reason

well, I'm sure there is one

"Grace"

"Amazing Grace" - the name of a song, and a poem that I did not write

Is it true, is it real, can it really be had

can we experience, or better yet possess, this unbelievable light

Sometimes the song makes me feel good,

sometimes I feel good anyway,

but not always

and I never feel that good, and I'm never content

because my good feelings are not permanent and they soon go away

I wouldn't know what to do if I always felt that well

I'd be scared at what was coming next, what's waiting to go wrong

but that's life here on earth, at least it is for me

I hope you fare well, and your life's good and long

But the real issue is in our future

and to me at least, this is uncertain

What is eternity, and who is it for

I expect it exists, but how will I know

and what should I do, what if I go wrong

can I make the wrong moves, and defeat my own purpose

can I even do right, or can I only do wrong

is it heaven I aim for, or is this not a reality

and how do I aim, is this within my ability

but again, I ask and I wonder, how do I know, what do I do

and then - aiming for heaven; is this appropriate, is it arrogant

could this be my downfall and elsewhere I go

Life after death, a question unanswered

and for me too scary to consider

so why do I mention it

good question

I guess I feel it's important

and I guess that I really want to know

so if there is salvation, and there really is this grace

then I hope that it finds all of us; all of you, all of me

and on current affairs, and the state of the nation

I can't answer all that, but I'll help if I can

and speaking of help

if I can ever have some, I ask that amazing grace is granted

and this will be my salvation

thank you God

"How does it look?"

If a person improves what they read
they may improve how they look
it's amazing what you can find
in the pages of a book

(look (in this case) is a verb; and in this case, a play on words)

"Inside" (to Hell with Temptation)

If it isn't inside, it doesn't exist

spend all your time chasing down

all that you can't resist

going all over the place,

need some of this, more of that

now look around, what did it get you

Take all your time and money, and life if you let it

but you can't live without and you cannot forget it

or can you?

of course you can

You've been around longer than that

you know better

now is no different, you've been there before

get back to your senses and do something about it

there's too much more than lousy temptation

where in the past have you found what you're looking for

think hard, use your head, use your reservations

what happened the last time you gave in to a craving

you wished that you hadn't, thought that was a mistake

here you go again

where will you end up this time

will you actually find anything that you're really looking for

or will you be set back even further from where you really want to go

how much life, time and money do you think it will take

but you don't even have to

you know that by now

you've done that before and you know what's the answer

so "to hell with temptation"

it's for you to decide

don't need and can't use it

if you can't find it inside

"Tabloid Nation"

Tabloid Nation

Freedom of the press

"There's something new to report"

from the spotlight arrest

presumed innocent

we know

but he's guilty

they've got him

the evidence is thick

it's enough to make you sick

The allegations are real

they were on CNN

the story, straight from the D.A.

all the networks and tabloids

and the L.A. TIMES

everything you need to know

and even more that you don't

about the unfolding story

of the L.A. crimes

All the media in the country

have been around and checked it out

the evidence tells the painful story

there isn't any doubt

the legal experts all agree

F. Lee Bailey

even me

It's obvious who did it

the evidence shows

there he is in handcuffs

everybody knows

a glove over here

a glove over there

something about a knit cap

with somebody's hair

he hid his hand in a gym bag

on a midnight flight

We've got that from several sources

so we know that it's right

there was blood all over the Bronco

that he took from the scene

then he put the bloody clothes

in his washing machine

the District Attorney says he acted alone

Kato says he wasn't home

they don't have the weapon

but they know where he bought it

anyway, the detectives have figured it out

no one else could have done it

he's the only one who had the time

seventy six minutes

to have committed this crime

it's a done deal

it's sealed

it's as sure as can be

the DA says "He'll take the insanity plea"

I've never seen so much focus

in just one case

news media and legal minds

from all over the country

just one mug shot

plastered all over the place

planted in your brains

the epitome of guilt

all you needed to know

but wait till you see this

they also have more

the forensics from the coroner

will be the final blow

soon we'll have every detail

it won't be that long

the District Attorney

and the tabloid media

couldn't be wrong

some people just think that it doesn't make sense

some people still wonder why

they had so much evidence in the first two days

almost all of it was wrong

in fact, it was a lie

did they fool the news media

or did the media fool you

and who gave these deceptive reports

anonymous sources

anonymous sources from where?

From Venus or Mars

or from Jupiter I suppose

or maybe the police

or the District Attorney

could it be, that these reports

have come from one of those

rarely have so many been fooled by so few

I guess you can just be glad

it wasn't you

or were these anonymous sources

here from the Moon

one thing is certain

the information

was fed with a spoon

when we allow liars and tabloids to prevail

expect the system of justice in America to fail

so keep it in mind

if evidence appears

and the truth survives through this mess

meanwhile proceed with caution

whatever you hear

what some people don't understand

and what some "legal experts" forgot

in America

the presumption of innocence

exists for a reason

if by slim chance, this country

can get around to it

they'll recognize the fact

that the possibility exists

that a person accused of a crime

didn't necessarily do it

The following is a copy of (most of) a letter that I wrote concerning the circumstances that inspired the above poem. I don't really know how many people will be that interested in this subject; however, I just thought I would include it for those who may be. It was written within a day or so of the poem in July '94. Some readers may well just want to skip the following paragraphs, but, it's up to the individual reader.

I have a concern for the way this scenario has taken place and the public perception of and reaction to it. I'm not trying to make a statement about innocence. I don't know and that's too long and involved to go into. And I have to remain open to accept what comes. But I'm concerned about the concept of the presumption of innocence and what gives police and prosecutors in Los Angeles the right to snuff it out.

I am concerned that the public is not concerned that they were lied to ("A ski-mask drenched in blood found at Simpson's estate" - verbatim from KCOP in Los Angeles and repeated on numerous occasions elsewhere across the country; Bloody clothes found in Simpson's washing machine; A vehicle of Simpson's found at his estate, awash in blood inside and out; A flight attendant and several passengers telling police and the Grand Jury that Simpson appeared shaken and nervous and appeared to be attempting to shield his left hand from view by keeping it submerged into a gym bag during his flight to Chicago; Simpson's house guest Kato telling police and the Grand Jury that Simpson had not been home on the night of the murders and showed up late only to catch the limo and go to the airport, contrary to what Simpson had told police).

All lies! It wasn't until Shapiro asked Clark at the hearing that we first found out that there was no bloody ski-mask. It wasn't till after the Grand Jury was disbanded that we found out that Kato had never testified that Simpson had not been home that night and in fact his testimony was that he and Simpson had gone to McDonalds and returned at 9:40 PM. We also didn't find out till after the Grand Jury that there had been no testimony from the flight attendant or passengers about Simpson nervous and shaken and hiding his hand in a gym bag (that's the one that convinced me). We didn't see pictures of the "Ford Bronco awash in blood" until the hearing where we needed a close-up from the court camera to view a close-up shot (a close-up of a close-up) of a spot of blood described as an eighth inch square-round above the door handle. If you dipped a Q-Tip in blood, you would have to shake it off, then gingerly dab it onto a surface, to get a spot that size (that small).

It is said that Simpson told police during his unrepresented interview with them that he sustained a small cut while packing his golf bag and may have transferred blood onto the Bronco while retrieving a cellular phone, this would make sense, but doesn't get mentioned very much.

The other night I was changing the flusher in my toilet and had the water to the house turned off (no shut-off valve at the toilet). At one point I grabbed a pair of hair-cutting scissors (sharp), to scrape some of the old plumbers goo from one surface and received a small cut on my finger (about an eighth inch straight-deep). Having the water turned off, I couldn't rinse it under the faucet, so I grabbed paper towels to wrap my finger and absorb the blood. I bled enough to drip a fair amount in the bathroom and put quite a bit on a number of paper towels over the next twenty minutes, then I grabbed an ice cube to stop the bleeding. I'm just saying this to illustrate that this small cut, (which none of my friends noticed the next day, until I pointed it out), would have left more than the amount of blood seen on the Bronco door or between the Bronco and Simpson's house. Neither would the loss of the amount of blood seen on the Bronco cause O.J. Simpson to bleed to death (refer to NFL tapes).

The reports of "bloody clothes found in Simpson's washing machine" were left to linger in the minds of the public for some time, and the prosecution never bothered to clarify that they didn't exist.

It bothers me greatly that the public doesn't appear to be upset about where these lies came from, or why they weren't set straight and it bothers me that despite the gradual unfolding of some truth, a great many people refuse to accept that there is no bloody ski-mask (at least not at Simpson's estate). Believe me, a great many people still have visions of bloody ski-masks, clothes in the washing machine, etc... I'm concerned about who planted these lies, who let them fester, that the public bought into them in the first place and that no one is bothered by the fact that they're lies, and that many people still see instant guilt and refuse to accept anything else.

I am also bothered by the fact that with all this, the commentary, continually faults Shapiro for using the media to his advantage with no reference to the mass brainwashing given the public in the first two weeks, which evidently worked. Shapiro didn't manufacture Fuhrman's statements in his lawsuit against the county - they exist. Fuhrman made them. People act like Shapiro made these statements up about Fuhrman and is trying to distract from the bloody ski-mask, etc.. This is backwards, Fuhrman made his own statements, they are real, there is no bloody ski-mask, somebody made that up.

What about that so called therapist, listed on TV as Nicole Simpson's therapist, who is said to have seen Nicole only two times, and may be looked at by psychiatric licensing board for discussing privileged client information on public television. She appeared numerous times on television and is quoted here "It's no mystery at this point in time, no secret; she was battered incessantly, regularly, all the time." I find this very hard to accept. Witness Simpson's size and strength. He could easily cause severe damage to a relatively strong and healthy man much larger than Nicole with only a couple of blows. If he hit her, I'm not defending it, I'm only saying that if he hit her hard a couple of times, it would cause broken bones if not brain damage.

Journalists do their profession and the public in general a disservice if they protect anonymous sources who feed viscous lies of this (or any other) magnitude. In fact they would do their profession a great service by letting the public and potential future sources know that anonymous sources that intentionally feed lies to the press/people will be exposed. If they did that then the press would not be abused in the future by liars and they would gain the public's trust that when they reference anonymous sources, they are credible sources.

These lies were introduced to the public as evidence (insurmountable) and left to fester for a long time and truths were withheld. Simpson may or may not be guilty. We don't know that. But we do know that someone or someone(s), basically brainwashed the country into visualizing his guilt. The Time and Newsweek covers with full page mug shots and reading "AN AMERICAN TRAGEDY" and "A TRAIL OF BLOOD", respectively, are right but they have the wrong understanding. The American Tragedy is the arrogance of the police and prosecution in L.A. and the ignorance of this country that the people were brainwashed and the entire TV and print media turned into tabloids. And the country into tabloid believers. There is a trail of blood, but no one is trying to find out what happened, they're simply trying to expand the tabloid coverage started in mid-June. The media wants pictures of the bodies; they're not concerned with who caused the deaths or who fed the lies to the press and public. Consider the reality of the circumstances that would have to have taken place for Simpson to have fulfilled all that happened in the 76 minute window of opportunity. Consider that any other possible perpetrator(s) had all the time in the world, because no one was tracing their movements before or after the crimes occurred. While the police scoured the area between Nicole's and Simpson's then went so far as to go to Chicago, they found no murder weapon(s), no clothes, shoes, etc..., Of course, had someone else committed the crimes, they had all the time and space in the world to get rid of this stuff, because no one was looking where they went.

I would find the first report of the glove found on Simpson's estate, I would be curious to see whether this report of a glove was accompanied by a report of "a ski-mask drenched in blood, or anything else." Who told this stuff to the media? What is the excuse for convincing the public of certain guilt when in fact it doesn't exist? There's not only no excuse, it should be considered a crime.

Bob Costas, Jack Kemp and others, respected people, long time friends and colleagues of Simpson's appeared on television in interviews and basically told of the good that they had known in Simpson, but basically appeared to be resigned to the "fact" that the "evidence against him" seemed to point to his guilt in these crimes. For weeks, people who knew and/or liked Simpson, had no choice but to accept that he must have done it. I've never been that big a fan of Simpson's but that's not the point.

I'm not certain what you'll think of what I'm saying, but I feel that these points and many more need to be made and I don't really know too many people who have too much of an interest and I just wanted to air my feelings.

It is my view at this point, that if Simpson is innocent that this case needs to be proven beyond any question against whoever did commit the crimes in order for him to escape being considered guilty by a good percentage of the public. And quite frankly, I believe that at this point there will still be many who think him guilty no matter what happens. I feel sorry for young kids.

I'm concerned about the effects no matter what the outcome of the trial. My reference to F. Lee Bailey (in the poem) is because prior to his and Dershowitz's joining the defense team, they had both been interviewed on television and made statements to the effect that the evidence appeared to be insurmountable. My point is that if these two were convinced by the "evidence" as introduced through the media, what are lay people to think? After these two joined the defense and started claiming 'presumption of innocence', many people saw it as just lawyers who would take big money and do anything to get their client off.

All of this doesn't even touch on the circumstances that would have to have occurred for Simpson to have pulled all this off between 9:40 and 10:55 and successfully disposed of the weapon(s), clothes, shoes, etc., changed and cleaned up to catch the limo. Conveniently leaving one glove at the crime scene and one at his house (banging on the wall of his house guest, to make sure someone would know to look out there). Both Kato and the limo driver testified that Simpson had no wound on his hand when they helped him pack the limo. Had he received that large wound during commission of the crime, he would have had to have doctored it pretty well between then and packing the limo so no one would have noticed. The limo driver testified that there were bags set outside when he arrived. When had Simpson set them out there? Add all this to what he did, between 9:40 and 10:55.

What kind of a homicide detective is Fuhrman if he had previously answered a 911 call in the past for domestic violence between O.J. and Nicole Simpson, he finds her and Goldman dead and doesn't even consider O.J. as a suspect, and then when he spots blood on Simpson's vehicle, he doesn't suspect that Simpson had been at the crime scene and transferred some blood from the scene, he sees an eighth inch square-round spot of blood and thinks *O.J.'s inside bleeding to death*. The only clue at the crime scene that would give the detectives any solid lead was one bloody glove (normally coming in pairs). Leaving the crime scene, the best thing that they could hope to find is the matching bloody glove. After searching the grounds at Simpson's, he and his penlight find a crumpled bloody glove in a darkened path and he notices that it's "similar in color and description to the glove at the crime scene." Who, under these circumstances, would notice or care about the color and description of a crumpled up bloody glove, found in a suspicious location. *A bloody glove is a bloody glove!* He testified that he accompanied the two lead detectives because he knew where Simpson's house was. They were referred to as the two top homicide detectives in Los Angeles. They couldn't find O.J. Simpson's house, two miles away? How do they answer 911 calls? I would like to ask all four detectives separately, whether they ever considered that Simpson may have been involved in the murders or not. Or whether when they saw blood on the Bronco they considered it or not. I would also like to ask them what scenario did they imagine that had O.J. not involved in the crime, but coincidentally inside bleeding to death. I simply can't imagine the country listening to this testimony and not being bothered by it.

I really apologize about the length of this letter, but I have tons of things on this subject that I feel are very troublesome and as I said, I really don't know too many people that are that interested so I wanted to air my feelings and I just hoped that you might have some agreement with my thinking.

As an after note, I want to add that, what I was trying to describe above is not to recommend that people should never speculate on ongoing crime scenarios. What I was concerned about and trying to describe above is separate from that.

"BTK Poem"

BTK
If I see you in hell
It'll be from a distance
If I see you in hell
I won't be there
I won't be there to greet you
In hell, I'll never meet you
You'll be on your own
There of your own volition
Enforced by your precision
Just as well
If at death, you emerge
from your cell
Following, that where you dwell
See you.....

"Drawing the Line"

You should have considered before you did that

You should have thought before you said what you said

I am easy going, but I'm drawing the line

Question my resolve and ability

Expect me to forgive and forget

Think that it doesn't matter

Assume that nothing is wrong

This is different

Test my conviction;

go ahead

Not all decisions are concrete

Adjusting for circumstances is virtuous and can lead to the best scenario

But there's a matter of right and wrong, and some rules must remain unbroken

Truth is paramount when dealing with life's matters,

before all things, this you must know

Go over the line

Cross my path

Test my conviction

Consider the situation and consequences

Go over the circumstances, consider your options

Know what you're dealing with before you take action

Think before you act, this time, use your head

Forgive you? that depends

Forget

I will not

You are responsible

Give it some thought

The difference between right and wrong is the difference

That's why you must understand

There is no compromise in this matter

What's right is right and what's wrong is wrong

the truth is the truth and that's all there is

You've seen it before so be certain this time

The difference is serious

That's why I'm drawing the line

"Consider the Long run"

I recommend you don't rush, and don't be so anxious
maybe even wait till you're older
I wouldn't want you to be sorry, or have to regret
in all things consider your sources
life may be short
but consider the long run
plan ahead in the things that you do
it's amazing what one person can do in a lifetime
count on this, you've much living ahead
In time you'll grow tired and feel overburdened
at times you might wish you could stop
you may take on too much and could be overwhelmed
times get hard and I'm afraid that you'll drop
give yourself time, think about what you're doing
seek advice, gain knowledge and grow
tackle all sorts of problems; figure everything out
trust me, you'll learn and you'll know
life itself is mammoth, and it's good to consider
the world in reflection is small
the world carries with it much substance
but look even further;
life itself carries all
Things don't always make sense, at least not to me
I attempt to observe and comprehend
gather views and advice from those you respect
share what you can with a friend
some things have no answers, this is a heartfelt belief
sometimes there's no consolation
and sometimes no relief

seems kind of silly, sounds stupid I guess

but for me, I know sometimes that life is a mess

we know that not everything's perfect

and too often not everything's clear

I really don't ask or expect much out of life

but it would be nice if we could

live our life without fear

life has its own schedule and many things are relative

sometimes things are better and sometimes they're not

what can an individual do to make things work in the long run

attempt what you can, think about it, work with what you've got

consider the possibilities and consider the results

consider all things affected

accomplishment is important, and consequences are significant

so when you act, remember, think ahead

this thing has no end, so where's the bottom line

if it were a conversation, I guess I could drop it

but in light of the circumstances, I've only one choice

make this the bottom line, and just stop it

"Spread a little life"

Spread a little life
that's what we can do
just a little more
a little for me, a little for you
a little here, a little there
a little more for someone else
some more for someone we don't know
a little more for myself
a little of yours, a little of mine
a little more on down the road
that way, just follow the sign

"Spend some time with Nature"

It can be hard to explain
things that people love most
or to describe the experience
when you get out into nature
like a trip to the mountains
or a trip to the coast
have crime and congestion overtaken the city
we all need a break, and a little simplicity
if concrete and congestion
make you cringe and complain
I have a suggestion
get away from the city
take a break; spend some time with nature
on the west coast, visit Washington
in the east, visit Maine

"Stand Tough"

Stand tough

Stand tall

Be fair

Be yourself

Keep the faith

Remember who you are

Do your best

Know your limits

Be honest

Don't let other people turn you around

"Do unto others, as you would have others

do unto you"

Fair winds and following seas

Be true to yourself

and always be strong

With all that you are

Don't be afraid

To admit when you're wrong

"It's the Meaning that matters"

It just doesn't rhyme, but that just doesn't matter

the words are just the means and the meaning is just that

it's the meaning, the meaning, the meaning, the meaning

The meaning, it's the meaning and that's what matters

But what does it matter; well you tell me

It depends on what it is, what it means and how much it matters

"Hours and Months"

April showers may bring flowers

but there's 12 months in a year

and so many hours

Each on their own, right down to the day

But they're also related, like April and May

So what does this mean and what should we do?

I can't say myself, but if you could tell me

I'd sure like to share it

This poem has no ending so why did I start it?

Just one of those things

what should I have done?

I'm sure it'll go somewhere, but I'm not sure I'll make it

if I get stuck for a rhyme, I suppose I could fake it

But life's not always like that

But sometimes it is

You don't have to know everything

or always be perfect

it's great if you do good

but sometimes you get stuck

sometimes good things just happen

but sometimes you're outta luck

but, so-what and who-cares and what's that got to do with the months of the year?

Well if it weren't for months and years we wouldn't have any time at all

where would we get summer, or of course spring and fall

and what about winter, I suppose it doesn't matter

But I bet some important things happen in each of these seasons

You should understand everything and know all of the reasons

Well, I guess that would be pretty hard to do

Be glad that you don't have to and that they're provided for you

So what do you make of it?

Make the best that you can

Can't always do that

But at least you have the time and opportunity

"It'll be the end of me"

There's no such thing as a good war
is that an opinion, or is that a fact
I'll just say that war itself isn't good
I'll just leave it at that
If this country's ever fought a good war
it was the one for independence
I must admit, I'm glad it happened
it allowed our country and people to live
it was the birth of freedom
if it's ever fought a wicked war
it would be the one that is known as civil
never again, the war between the states
that one should not have ever happened
it should never have been done
the concept of slavery is so obviously wrong
they should not have had to fight to end it
way too many people died
it went on for too long
and then the war to end all wars
the big one, world war one
it's much too serious, the loss too great
how could we survive, but what else could we do
and then too soon, more war to come
the other war to end all wars, the other big one
world war two
and then Korea
and then Viet Nam
it's too much, we can't go on
don't say it was a police action

don't say it wasn't a war

each person has but one life to give

you can't give any more

there's only one way to win a war

and if it comes to war, you want to win

strategy to win must be thorough from the start

be prepared before you begin

don't ever go in undecided

if you go into battle

don't straddle the fence

have your cause and your goals

outlined and determined

take it seriously, our national defense

peace through strength, would be the way to go

if indeed peace is to be gained

if not, a quick and decisive victory

should always be attained

don't screw around,

don't play politics

war is hell, war is war, get it over

don't drag it out, you want this one over and done

could it happen again

what would be the reason

will there be more to come

another war to end all wars

could it happen, how could it be

if there ever is another world war

could we bring a quick and decisive end

don't screw around if there has to be

another big one

a world war three

"Ladybug"

Don't ever kill a ladybug, don't you dare
God will turn you to stone and He'll mess up your hair
He'll make you walk alone in the cold
and if you think that's not fair
He'll play games with your mind
and He'll make you grow old
"Oh the misery, the bad luck, this dreaded existence
what ever could I have done to receive such a fate
when all along I should be at home
with loved ones around me
and all safe and snug"
But it's all unnecessary
It could be avoided
so be careful of hate
and above all
what ever you do
take note of your behavior
and Don't ever kill a Ladybug

"Missed the Train"

I've missed the train and now it's lost
it doesn't pass this way again
its course is set
its destination in place
there is no chance
for me to get aboard
I'm not left totally without
or abandoned
or defeated by any means
however I must regroup
and rethink my intentions
I could probably survive
in a number of ways
some certainly better than others
I simply won't have the benefit
of that particular resource
however, if I stop and think
and apply myself to the situation
I can certainly adapt
and find another course

"Spider Webs and Moonlight"

Spider webs and Moonlight

Planets and Stars

Blue skies and Evergreens

Clean air and cars

Far from the maddening

or caught up in a crowd

the Sun is shinning all the time

Somewhere, there're always clouds

"I have a mouse in my pocket"

I have a mouse in my pocket, so don't cross my path
you'll stir up my dander and encounter my wrath
My mouse is a good one and he protects only me
he'll teach you a lesson you couldn't foresee
You cannot escape him, despite what you think
he's fast and he's smart, you'll loose in a blink
My mouse is automatic, he'll strike you post-haste
he'll uncover your weak spots and lay you to waste
First he'll crack all your knuckles and bite on your toes
then he'll buckle your kneecaps and feed on your nose
You'll want only mercy, unable to cry
and he'll attack with his whiskers and tickle your eye
My mouse is a good one and he helps me so much
he's enlightened my life and enhanced my own touch
In a moment of passion he'll get you alone
and give you a pointer to help out your cause
You'll wonder what he's up to; will he strike you again?
Is it a ploy? are you outsmarted? he's not even a man
You're afraid you can't trust him, he's got you alone
then he shows you something; - a little funny-bone
He comes from a good family and was raised on a farm
my mouse couldn't really do anyone harm
He's there just to help you, there's nothing to fear
he doesn't even speak but his message is clear
My mouse knows English, and science and math
he anticipates needs and he finds you a path
If you think you know something he doesn't, - just stop!
you won't overcome him, he stays well on top

You'll practice and learn and with all that you do

he'll quickly inform that he's smarter than you

He knows what you want and he'll help you to see

Trust me; my mouse runs my computer and he's smarter than me

"For the People"

Over two centuries have passed, and many generation

Not the beginning of time, but, the beginning of a nation

The country was born, with an act from above

Earth, wind and fire and steel forged with love

The true pioneers, as we call them today

a new world beginning, they'd come here to stay

"We'll build houses and roads, and have cattle and farms"

"We'll need teachers and schools; strong minds and strong arms"

Sun up and sun down, the earth steadily turned

so much to be done, so much to be learned

"We'll need taxes and laws, but we won't need this tea"

"We'll have a constitution"; "We'll have to be free"

"Of the people, by the people and for the people"

one man, one vote

"All men created equal"

one person wrote

The Indians suffered and so too the black

wrongs can be righted, but they can't be taken back

Independence and civil war

Can this country survive?

The world still turns

Freedom is still alive

From all ends of the earth

the one melting pot

We've fought and we've died

to have and have not

Through history we've come and through history we'll go

Trials and fears, over miles, over years

One country so great, bearing so much respect

There has to be government; we have to elect

Can honesty and character keep us on the trail?

Could corruption and greed cause us to fail?

America exists, by the sword and the pen

and for leaders we're looking,

for a few good men

"Back to Normal"

So it's back to normal

whatever that is

a good question in itself

I'm not certain now that I even remember

I suppose I might wonder if I ever knew

or actually, I now wonder, is there a normal; how can you tell

is normal perception

is normal relative

Normal in relation to what

there's a question

This is all just for the sake of conversation

or thought maybe

Just fun I guess

no real deep meaning

I suppose if you tried to get too serious about anything in life

you could cause yourself considerable grief

I've been told many times that I'm too serious

I disagree

though there may be something to it

I have often thought that other people weren't serious enough

I suppose it's a matter of perception

and I suppose it's relative

but enough of that and back to normal

Here we go again

is it necessary that I comprehend normal

It must not mean anything or make any sense

I could get serious about this and go on forever

try to figure out everything and cause myself grief

or maybe save some of my sanity

and not worry too much about it

I think I'll do that

In this case, I'll be brief

that's it

back to normal

"New World Order" (Damn Fools and Communists)

On this earth where I stand, is a once familiar land

reality is the truth that I fear

the world is now one, no more homeland

and to think, that it happened right here

the people are here, but life's gone from their face

The *new world order* is now in place

I regret every minute and every second

and I regret every heartbeat and breath

every ounce of sweat and strength that was wasted

as I neglected to fight to the death

from the U.S. Marines to Nevada's wild horse

It's all gone now, taken by force

with a gun to my head I observe the new flag

Old glory is now dead and gone

where America once was

we now have a new cause

and quite frankly, we're better off dead

we've received a new set of values

and have been handed a new set of rules

If you'd have seen us before, you would never have thought

that we'd turn out to be, such a bunch of damn fools

what existed before has now been smashed

along with the lives we once had

as we thought among our selves and we wondered

could this new world order, really be so bad

how could America, have ever been so blind

the cornerstone of freedom and life

what were our thoughts, as our destiny approached

as the enemy within, divided and encroached

one world order is now what we've got

exist in this new world, - I might

but as I still have heart, and I still have a mind

pledge allegiance to the flag, - I will not

"The Pied Piper of Washington"

The pied piper of Washington, influential you bet,

he'll wine and he'll dine you, corner and sign you and he'll tell you who to respect

follow his lead - bid his will, accept what he says, advance his cause and yours

his power will feed you, he really does need you, don't ignore him and do not neglect

devote attention and resources, spend time and money,

don't worry he'll show you the way

act at our peril, you are not responsible, you'll gain and you will get away

improve your own life, be good to your self, the burden will not fall on you

you will not account, it's others who suffer, don't worry, you'll gain,

someone else has to pay

Don't have a conscience; you'll loose your feeble mind

you just couldn't live with yourself

what will become, if you ever grow up

consider the trouble you'll find

You're fine as it is, nothing will stop you

the world is at your disposal

but should you wake up, and your conscience come alive

then I have a serious proposal

look closely at yourself, examine what you are

where you came from, and what you've become

then consider the others, whose lives you affect

take a strong look and see what you've done

have you helped anyone, have you done any good

what really in life is your cause

or who have you harmed, who suffers the loss

do you cheat; do you break any laws

the issue is not simple, life is not short, tell me, do you have a friend

ask his true feelings, evaluate yourself, what will you be in the end

"A Reminder and a Note" (to all enemies, foreign and domestic)

A simply stated message, easy to comprehend

a reminder and a note

about our history

and the future of our land

The time is now, the people are here

The message and the goal, are true and are clear

Should anyone consider us unable, and expect us to fail

Think again

This is America

It will not be lost and it isn't for sale

Born of the American Revolution

written in our constitution

As the Liberty Bell and freedom ring

on this nation is our life preserved

It's the land of the free and the home of the brave

the land of "liberty or death" and much more

It's the home of Old Glory, old mountains and farms

freedom of speech, freedom of press and the right to bear arms

So I offer these thoughts, with pen in hand

Watch us grow, as together we band

observe our strength, and please, understand

This is America, this is our home

and united we stand

"What's the Season?"

Time is upon us, and we have reached the season

America's age is prophetic and ripe

Observe the shine of the sun and the fall of the rain

recall the song, the spacious skies and the amber waves of grain

Take stock in your memory and what you hold dear

Take heed of your surroundings and that which you fear

Stick to your guns and don't surrender you arms

Take note in the cities and keep hold of your farms

Consider your family and that which you love

the time is arriving, of the hawk and the dove

The fruits of your labor and the seeds that you've sewn

are enhanced by your country and the freedom you've known

Take care, take light, it's your world, you're the one

Give strong thought to your past and the things that you've done

There's one life and it's yours, so don't give it away

Take strength in your self and the life of the day

Consider your people and life as you know it

Call life as you see it

Let truth be your guide

Don't give up the ship or your life

but remember the past and take note of the season

know that where evil grows it must have a seed

Don't give freedom away and remember this

The quote of a poet and a book that I want you to read

"Treason doth never prosper, what's the reason

for if it prosper, 'None Dare Call it Treason'"

None dare call it treason, but that's what it is

treason, treason in the highest form

expect it, and believe, it will be done very well

it will come under the heading - "government reform"

The heart of the country beats within you

and the essence of life is yours alone

If the land is still ours, and we own our own cars

then hold on to your reason and the seeds that you've sewn

"Don't give up the ship"

Society's sunk, it's become a lost cause
we've become a damn nation of mutilated laws
too much to go into, no sense in spelling it out
but just let me ask you, what would you say, this world's all about
I can't watch the news anymore, we're all better off dead
I'm still bent out of shape, from some things that I've read
It's all been deranged or perverted, murdered or messed up
defiled or distorted, crimed or corrupted
Can't tell them that, who ever the hell they may be
they all know better and they never shut up
try to point out what's right, make improvement or teach some respect
they either can't understand or they just refuse to see
try to say something important and you get interrupted
So what do we do, what's next, you tell me
no sense in trying to lead a constructive life
someone with nothing better to do is sure to come along and screw it all up
society's a loss and then there's our government
let's all pay more in taxes, might as well, can't afford anything else
so where does it come from and what do we do
who is responsible, is it just me and you
you can't teach a lesson to someone who doesn't care
or teach right and wrong to someone who doesn't understand
what would possess someone and how can they live like that
where did they come from and will they ever learn
or is it too late, will we never regain sanity
will our lives be lost to other's perversion and corruption
their greed and immorality,
their lousy mistakes and irresponsibility
their crime and their vanity

There's so many good people, but where can you find them

They're busy fighting crime or corruption or they're afraid to come out

the world's gone to hell and I'm tired as well

no motivation to fight this immovable force

but I'm not alone, or am I

No, I think not, there are many others of course

it's just that the bad ones take up all the time and money

let me guess, you want it to stop, you think it's not funny

Good people make the world go around

but bad people get all the publicity, screw things up for the rest of us

and take up all of the tax dollars

So the question comes again, what do we do

I don't have the answers but I'll help if I can

and I'll make a couple of suggestions

those who can read and comprehend

consult your conscience and your heart for strength and guidance

seek views, advice and opinions from good people and those that you trust

a general acknowledgment that something is wrong

it's too obvious now and it's gone on for too long

don't shrivel at the challenge, you're not the only one

 we don't have the answers but something needs to be done

If you have a chance, do your part; teach reason and respect

be strong with a heart, correct immorality and irresponsibility

take it all on yourself, go ahead, do it all

collect all the problems, take responsibility and carry the world on your shoulder

just kidding

but do your part if you want to live well and be at peace when you're older

But there are no answers, unless God will provide them

that's my feeling and of course I may be wrong

but meanwhile I'll try to do my part and add to what's right and sometimes when I think I can't function

I can't find salvation or consolation in the efforts I make

I'll retreat for a time and maybe learn something

listen to some good jazz, classical, oldies, elevator or other music

maybe read or think, talk to a friend or relative or listen to talk radio

and at times I'm sure that I'll just shake my head

stay home, do some thinking, and listen to the Grateful Dead

but don't give up

"Drive" - "Something to think about"

If you think before you drink

you probably won't

If you think you need a drink

you probably don't

If you drink and then you forget how to think

you probably shouldn't

If you think it's ok to drink and then drive

please think again

I wouldn't

If you're concerned about yourself and the others

who are doing their best to survive

just remember the lines from the old days

they're easy to remember

and they should make you think

IF YOU DRINK - DON'T DRIVE

IF YOU DRIVE - DON'T DRINK

"A Clean Shot"

Can't get a clean shot

Can't take it easy

Can't do much of anything the way that I'd like to

I'd like to be more productive

and do great and wonderful things

I'd like to be better

but I guess that I'm not

"The Spirit of Cooperation"

The goal is world peace, peace and prosperity

we've only had it once before, so it must be a genuine rarity

No wait, I take that back, we've never had it

never had it at all

well that's not very good

that's no good whatsoever

So what in the world do we do

well that's a good question

I'm certain that I don't have an answer

though I do think about it at times

so I suppose that if I don't do anything else

I might as well make a suggestion

Maybe a couple, as a matter of fact

But they wouldn't do any good, I'm certain of that

It's just something to think about

I'll bet before I was done

I could come up with several

at least more than one

I think the fundamental problem

with the entire situation

Is that everyone would have to agree

or at least they'd have to cooperate

To attain world peace

you'd have to have concurrence

most importantly you need some real cooperation

Let me know when you get it; I'll be there to help

Cooperation will be the hard part

I think that's the main problem

without concurrence and cooperation there is no peace

what you will have will be varying degrees of disorder

you have either disorder or you have domination

nobody likes domination; at least no one I know

In general, people want their own way, to some extent or another

but everyone can't have it, things just don't work that way

people disagree all the time, even sister and brother

that seems to be the way it is, but things usually work out somehow

not always though, that's for certain

too many people want to be the boss

they think that someone else should be the one to take the loss

cooperation can often require sacrifice

to some degree or another

if everyone were fair, things would be easier in general

people could get along pretty well with each other

and probably things would be pretty nice

what's all this got to do with the goal of world peace

As long as there's one people who want to dominate another

world peace will not come, I guarantee you that

the will of God and the spirit of cooperation

are this world's only hope

with as much concurrence as possible,

and a certain amount of sacrifice

fair play and a few other ingredients, everyone's better off

it's easier to cope

If we can't attain world peace I guess,

we should concentrate on ourselves

our personal and professional relationship's,

and how we get along

with everybody else

whether it's world peace or not; whatever the situation

I think one of the best things we can do among ourselves

is to understand, practice, and if we have a chance, spread

the spirit of cooperation

"Space"

"Stay there"
I said
to an empty space
"stay there"
I said to a space that was empty
what possessed me to speak
with no one else around
what is this space
that I thought I had found
"good deal, it's still there," I said
as I approached even nearer
traveling backwards
looking in my rear-view mirror
there's no real need to race
there's no one else around
just what I was looking for
in a parking place

"The Superior Mind"

You have a superior mind, whoever you are
what a fine mind it is
superior indeed
just look at yourself and the things that you've done
why it's amazing to think that you have only one
who would have thought that you could do all of that by yourself
I'm awestruck and don't know what to say; I'm impressed
I like what you've done and think you should be proud
that's something to feel good about; 'cause you're a decent person
Rainbows and Pots-o-Gold, life is more often not
but I like people like you, and the things that you do
and I'm impressed, with the mind that you've got
I actually think that yours is a superior mind
I guess that's what God gave to his people
mankind
and I think your mind is superior, whoever you are
superior indeed, superior by far
I saw the Northern Lights tonight
Tonight I saw the Northern Lights

"Simplicity"

Simplicity, the age old key
the only one there is
the key that's been around for so very long
while other keys have come and gone
the original design of the world worked so well
can not really be improved
works so well because it's round
spherical, if you must
but a better design has not been found
the original is the one you can trust
you could complicate just about anything
I could complicate this silly little poem, if I wanted
but, complication doesn't accomplish
so if possible it should be prevented
so how do you prevent complication
it should be relatively easy
if you stick with your age old key

"The American Wasteland"

The American wasteland, Washington D.C.

what a fascinating place this is

just full of all sorts of important people

uncounted interesting things

important events, even foreign affairs

just an incredible array, including all sorts of biz

Who are these people and what is their purpose

what do they do, what is their meaning, and what do they want

Are they important, are they serious

Do they know what they're doing

Do they accomplish their goals

are they good, are they funny

What does it mean to you and me

What is their effect on our lives and our family

Do they improve our lives, do they help us survive

do they do any good for our families and business

and why is it, do you suppose, that they want all of our money

Do they use it to maintain their offices and cars

Do they use it to pay for their consultants and staffs

So how is your office and how is your staff

You say you can't really afford one, you have to do without

Tell me, does this make you angry or does this make you laugh

You say that you've sent all your money to Washington

D.C. says they need it and they say that you don't

You say this time next year you'll be fresh out altogether

When they ask you for more, you will try but you won't

have any money, at least not much

What you had went to pay for your taxes and debt

and so now you're without and you collect unemployment

and it's not very much that you get

So you don't know what to do but you're looking at welfare

It's not what you want but you don't see a choice

What do you mean, you don't like BIG GOVERNMENT

What do you mean that they don't seem to care

you want to tell them

you could explain it so well

You've tried to get through, but they won't hear your voice

But BIG GOVERNMENT is doing very well "thank you very much"

They have programs and studies and cabinets,

and lawyers and consultants and staffs

They get good pay and retirement, they travel and have perks

They have nice cars, their own boats and nice houses and such

So who are you to be complaining

It's BIG GOVERNMENT that's important, not you

But if the tables were turned they would do some explaining

They'd have to account for the things that they do

So sue them

but you can't, and it's true that they don't

account for themselves or take responsibility

You'd like to make *them* pay, but they're far out of reach

and they are immune so it's beyond your ability

You see, you say, you're on an unfixed income

You've lost your faith and all of your rights and the government is too big

They're like communists or socialists and they fill you with smoke

Now they're doing so well and you're on an unfixed income

in other words; now BIG GOVERNMENT is doing fine

and the American people, are all broke

"If it wasn't for your Birthday" (Happy Birthday to a Parent)

If it wasn't for your birthday

you would never have gotten anywhere

as a matter of fact

neither would I

if it wasn't for your birthday

all sorts of things would never have happened

take me for instance

I would never have learned

how to get around very well

or how to drive a car

in fact, I would have never been born

so I certainly would never have gotten very far

I would never have learned how to read or to run

heck, I couldn't even crawl, I wouldn't have any fun

If it wasn't for your birthday

just think of all that we would have missed

my brothers and sisters

and who knows what else

never had a friend

or never been kissed

so for all the things

that never would have happened

I think that your birthday's a pretty important date

so I have a proposal

let's celebrate

or at least let me say

once again, "thanks to you and - Happy Birthday"

"Watch it Unfold"

So what is your age, and what are you doing?

what have you learned and where have you been?

what are your interests, and what your concerns?

are you content, doing well, is everything ok?

what are your plans and what your intentions?

consider your options, look at the possibilities

call up your memory, evaluate the past

examine what actions attain what results

there's much room to grow

but there's also room for error

some you can afford but avoid the big mistake

caution and consideration should pay off in the long run

advancing with care will get you further

than making up for bad judgment

so consider your future, all it will be

look where you are now and where you have been

what remains is unseen, but it is yours to see

so look now at your life; watch it unfold

so what will you do, when you're sixty years old

"Where Found?"

Where do you find beauty………?
Is it in the eye of the beholder…...?
What does that mean?
You tell me

"What do you want?"

You don't know what you've got till it's gone
so how do you know what you want,
till you have it
then it's gone

"Why Meditate"

Meditate, meditate and nothing else matters

Meditate now, and don't look back

Meditation; is that the answer

I don't know, I really don't

will it help, I don't know

will it hurt, I think not

but what if it does

then don't do it

if it helps, take advantage and gain

if it hurts, like I say, don't do it

stay away and consider other things

avoid pain and mistakes,

like the kid, who gets away from the stove when it's hot

I may well be wrong, and I really don't know

but I would think that meditation could be good

I don't know myself, and I can't do it either

but I've tried it before and I expect that I'll try it some more

Why meditate, well, I won't say why not

but I think to enhance concentration and thought

hopefully to better understand

if you understand perfectly well already

and if you concentrate as well as you could

then maybe there's nothing to gain, at least not for you

but if you could gain, then maybe you should

what is meditation, anyway

good question, and I don't have that answer

but I like the thought of it and some people say

meditation is good and there's also the saying

meditation is kinda like prayer

Do you have all the answers and know everything

would you do me a favor and tell me

please

if not would you please at least answer a question when I ask

or if nothing else don't lie or mislead me

what's that got to do with meditation

what's meditation got to do with life

I've read a description of meditation in a book

the author says "it's like going home"

I like that description and I'd like to achieve that end

but I doubt if I ever will

but I like to think about it

and I thought that if nothing else

I could at least tell you and I could at least write this poem

so what's the deep meaning and the answers

and where's the incredible truth

got me

If I knew, I'd tell you

I've read a couple of books on meditation

I'm looking for advanced relaxation, concentration

I haven't fount it but that shouldn't stop you

and I have found some comfort in the pages of the books

"How to Meditate" and "Finding the Quiet Mind"

those are the names and I'm sure that there's more

but I hesitate to go too deep into something

that could mislead my direction

or cause me the wrong thing to find

so these books just tell a little about meditation

and give some background and experience and stuff

I would think if done right, meditation could sure help

a little insight and comfort when you need it

when answers don't seem to be forthcoming

and anxiety appears to have taken over

forget the past and other problems

and don't worry about the future

at least not this minute

let the world take care of itself for a while

your life, the world and all these people

the people, the world and your life and everything in it

try not to worry too much

concentrate on yourself

will it get you anywhere, can you do anything

I don't think that's necessarily the goal

I believe it's a matter of your self

the who, what and why of your soul

just kidding

that's too deep

and I don't seek those answers

I basically seek to get along

try to do what's right, when I can and I know what it is

and use caution and try to avoid what is wrong

So does this bunch of stuff really mean anything

I wouldn't let it mean too much

don't let anything consume your life or what's good about it

you figure most of it out by yourself

but good advice and opinion and experience can be good

and if meditation or conversation or simply good reading can help

then use it, if you think that you should

The above mentioned books are "Finding the Quiet Mind"
by Robert Ellwood. Published by Quest.
"How to Meditate" by Lawrence Le Shan. Published by Bantam.

"All that you are"

All that you are…
is all that there is……..
kinda

"Until Then"

Prayer and meditation,
prayer and meditation
I need answers
can I find them there
I don't have the answers
I haven't found them
But I can honestly say that I've tried
and I hope that the answers will come
and I hope that I will have peace
when I can no longer look
and I've run out of steam
when at last
I finally have died
Until then...

"From Within"

Whole human beings
destroyed from within
never will find
where they wanted to go
find themselves stranded
left to do without
forgot where they were going
and don't know why
don't know what they're missing
just really don't know
used to have something better
but now that's gone
thought they'd found something
and don't know what went wrong
whole human beings
dcstroycd from within
because of alcohol and drugs
it really seems a sin

"Ulterior Motives"

Ulterior motives, the root of all evil?

but then, when I think further, it all comes back to ego

I don't know if this is right, certainly can't say it's fact

but thinking on somewhat, it occurs to me that

it's worth thinking over, some consideration is due

I have some opinions, I expect you have some too

there've been several suggestions, some say this or that

money, greed, sex, power, have I left something out

I'm sure there are more, and I expect more to come

the combined roots of all evil, maybe more than just one

who knows, some people care, I'm sure all have some base

whatever it is, I expect the root of all evil, would be hard to erase

maybe if it's identified, it would be easier to spot

but then what would we do? Could we wipe it all out

doubt it, but we could try, it'd be nice to find out

but then back to the subject, what's the name of this root

I'll bet I could list more, and then more to boot

Let's take a shot, take a chance, take a shot in the dark

name it once and for all, and make a good mark

the roots of all evil, all rolled into one

so we can spot it and kill it and then there'll be none

so consider all the possibilities and how to combine them

what do they have in common, where can you find them

so does it have a label this root of all evil

I'll take my best shot and say it all comes from ego

"One Big Word"

Encyclopedia, now that's a big word
a conglomeration of information
a place to look up, to read, and learn
and find out more about,
some of the things that you've heard
not everything's in there
but there sure is a lot
find out about all sorts of things
whether you have to or not
you can't learn everything from the encyclopedia
or anywhere else as far as I know
but what would you do if you knew everything
where would you go
I guess you don't have to answer that
but if you knew everything you could
but if you don't there's always the encyclopedia
and of course, that's only one of so many places to learn
but if you get to a point where you think you know everything
I think you ought to make certain
just in case you're mistaken; you should always double check
but where would you double check to make sure you know everything
well if you're not certain, exactly where to check it out
then you might be mistaken, if you still have some doubt

I think it's not likely that you'll know exactly everything

I suspect that would be hard to do

and then if you forgot something

or something changed,

you'd have to start over again

but most people seem to manage, knowing a certain amount

and who knows everything

I guess we could always ask who

"Poetry in Motion"

Poetry in motion
not really
static words
with a certain flow
ink on paper
observed by the mind
where does it go
what to you find

"Twilight Zone"

Insanity Reigns

just look at the news

crime and corruption all over

deception, murder and so much more

perversion and pornography; what else

more death and deception

more corruption and crime

where are we going from here

and do we have to

trouble in the streets

and then there's the television

you can see more perversion

at home in prime time

adultery, abuse

what perversions don't we have

or should I wonder, what's going right

reality is one thing, but this stuff's insane

you may not agree

but then again, you might

the difference is lost between right and wrong

the government's a mess and then there's the debt

no quick fixes for problems that have grown to such proportions

you can pay more in taxes, but what will you get

but back to the streets and corruption and crime

kids with guns, drugs and car-jackings

illegitimacy, abuse and irresponsibility abound

more to list, and I'm sure more to come

I suppose I could spell it all out

make some suggestions

but that's been done before, so I wonder

what's the use

sex sells

it also causes problems

it's a leading cause of adultery, AIDS, illegitimacy,

sex abuse, abortion, teen pregnancy and prostitution

sex, drugs and rock and roll

idiots in charge and that's not all

these damn people seeking their fortune and fame

so many things wrong but no one's to blame

between government and television, we don't stand a chance

sanity does not rule these institutions

so it's into semi-hibernation

escape this reality if I can

for a while at least

but I'll still watch the news

you'll see me again, when sanity rules

"Utopia"

When you get to Utopia, look me up
I'll be there, in my easy chair
it's not at all like this
it's better by far
the atmosphere is pleasant indeed
no matter who you are
I'm certain you'll like it
it's easy to find
Utopia my friend
exists in your mind
but as far as the world
in which we live
as we search for our favorite
part of the sphere
I'll tell you so far, from what I've found
I tend to favor, what we have right here
though it takes some effort to pay the bills
and assorted other social ills
I haven't been all places
but from what I can see
America's the best around

"Cats & Ducks"

If it looks like a duck
It might be a cat
But, probably not
Something like that

"If it looks like a duck" - Letter to the Editor 1993

The recent materialization of middle class tax cuts, which came in the form of "Everything that you own or don't own, earn or don't earn, do or don't do" is now taxable and the renaming of the American system of taxation as "sacrifice" or "contribution" or "patriotic act" depending on which day you tuned in, reminded me of some arguments that took place on the floors of government several years ago. The argument was whether or not there was a tax involved in some act or another and although I really don't remember it very well I remember news clips of one or more lawmakers trying to make their point by referring to the old saying "if it looks like a duck, walks like a duck, quacks and swims like a duck, then it's probably a duck".

Aggravated as these arguments seemed at the time, the current attempt at taxing the American people and making them believe that they are not being taxed, makes that time period seem like the good old days of simplicity.

I sent the above paragraphs and poem to the two Seattle newspapers as a letter to the editor, knowing well that they wouldn't print it, but I wish I could have seen the looks on the faces of whoever read it. I just thought it was funny, so I included it.

"If it looks like a Duck, it must be a Rose" (or is it my cats) - "The renaming of America"

A rose by any other name

Here in America, where this beauty achieved her great fame

We need not your beauty now Rose; just send us the fax

and by the way young lady,

you're now officially a tax

Afterword

While I have never really had a strong personal interest in poetry, I have appreciated certain poetry over the years when I had come by it. And, I have always had an appreciation for well written lyrics. The first thing that I wrote here didn't start out as poetry. It was late evening, overnight and I was listening to a talk radio program that I used to listen to which started at midnight. At the time, the radio program was mainly based on politics and news of the day. This evening, was overnight New Year's Eve, 31 Dec '92 - 1 Jan '93; I'm pretty certain that one caller was former Speaker of the House, Tip O'Neill. I only heard a part of the conversation and I believe I recognized his voice. In either case; whether he was the caller or not; the conversation got me thinking about politics. On the subject, I was thinking of how profoundly the country can be affected by the Congress. At some point, I had some thoughts that I wanted to get into notes, in order that at some point, I may be able to write some form of paper that would express what I considered the profound significance of Congress. I got up and went to my computer, and started trying to think of a format and to jot down notes which I wanted to eventually tie together into a basic paragraph format. At first, I had jotted down several notes, and then, I started just writing down thoughts in basic bullet format. Then, kind of before I knew it, I was just starting to somehow tie various lines together and using rhyme in the process. At some point, I felt I could see a concept developing; I took it from there and basically worked on completing the writing in poetry format. This was the first thing that I had written in this format, with the exception of maybe something from grade school or whatever. This became what I now call "For the People" which I had also, at one point called "The Nation, the People, Democracy and the Constitution" and which I also or at least almost called "A Few Good Men" based on the last line of the poem. This was coincidentally, around the time frame of the movie "A Few Good Men" and I wasn't sure if it was a good idea to use that as a name.

The following days, weeks and months, for the next couple of years, I found myself utilizing the concept and writing down various thoughts in similar format. This basically resulted in the contents of this book.

With some of the poems here, the reader may wonder, where I am coming from, or who I am talking to, or what inspired a particular subject. Well, it's kind of hard to explain. Basically in some, it is a form of what I call 'thinking out loud on paper' which is just a way of expressing some things that some others may, or may not relate to. If there are certain poems that a reader does relate to, but also, some that they don't, then they can simply disregard the ones that they really don't appreciate. Nothing here should be taken that seriously or is intended to be that significant.

I am struggling with whether it's a good idea or not to try and add a few afterword notes concerning some of the material in the book. There are a couple of poems that I also struggle with whether to leave them in or take them out of the book. But, at this point, I really can't see myself taking any of them out. There are a few, but not many, already that are not included. The reader will find that there are some poems which have very similar themes and even some repeated lines. But, that's just the way they came out; so, I've just left them as they are.

The poem "Tabloid Nation" was written in July of '94 concerning the fiasco surrounding the arrest of O. J. Simpson. Following the poem, I included several paragraphs of a letter that I had written to my Uncle at the time, concerning the circumstances. As I'm writing this, in December of '08, O.J. Simpson is again in the news and has just been sentenced in Las Vegas. The poem "Tabloid Nation" and the following paragraphs are not statements on the innocence or guilt of Simpson. I have no comment on that subject. They are statements on the circumstances surrounding the crime and the coverage and the police and the public's attitude, mainly concerning the 'presumption of innocence.' Frankly, most people can just skip the paragraphs following the poem, unless you happen to be interested in the subject. It really shouldn't be taken too seriously. I was just throwing out something to consider. Some may find it interesting; many may not. As I mentioned following the paragraphs, I'm not intending to recommend that there should be no speculation concerning current, outstanding crimes.

Two poems basically are based on the theme of government conspiracy and it's occurred to me that some may wonder just how seriously I consider this issue. "New World Order" or "Damn Fools and Communists" and "What's the Season" Frankly, I don't personally consider that there really is any government conspiracy; however, I've read some and heard discussion on the issue, mainly, back around the time frame that these were written. I feel that it's healthy for the nation to be vigilant concerning the growth of government and the maintenance of Constitutional and civil rights by the people. I suppose that I should just say that, these poems were written in order to express the attitude that I would take, if I thought there were government conspiracy.

The BTK Poem, is in reference to the BTK serial killer of Wichita, KS; who has since been apprehended. I had posted in on a BTK discussion board.

Almost all the material here was written in 1993 and 1994. Mostly in '93 and only a few in 1995 or after. I never got around to getting them copyrighted till I sent them in, in September of '07 and received the copyright in 2008. I frankly never had the time or opportunity to get all things organized and do all that I had to do, proofreading, etc, in order to put it all together. At this point I hope to have them self-published, through Author House in early 2009. With very few exceptions, none of the material in this book has been shared with anyone else. I have shown one or two of the poems to one or two friends or family members, a long time ago, but, not much. By the way, about proofreading; I have only proofread this myself; no one else has looked at it. This is a self-publishing project. I hope I didn't make any too embarrassing mistakes. As I sometimes tell people that I correspond with by email "please excuse any miscellaneous typos, etc…"

Here I am including a copy of the table of contents with the dates the various poems were written. I don't know how significant that is to anyone else; but, I like to have it here for reference. Many only list the month and the year because, I didn't write down the specific date, when it was written, but, I noted the general time frame. Some, simply are listed as 1990s in which case they would all be 1993 or after.

"Table of Contents"

Acknowledgements/attributes/citations

In an abundance of caution, I want to identify the few instances in my poems where I have, to whatever extent, quoted or mentioned another author.

I titled one poem "Bang the Drum Slowly" which is also the first line. Frankly, at the time I wrote it; I had no idea where I had become familiar with that phrase. In fact, I just looked it up on Google, and as far as I can tell per Wikipedia, the original use was for a novel by that name by Mark Harris, first published in 1956.

In the poem I call "Impossible Dream" the first two lines are "The Impossible Dream" (and) "The unreachable star" The title and these lines are inspired by the song "The Impossible Dream" Lyrics written by Joe Darion.

In the poem "What's the Season?" – I mention the name of a book "None Dare Call it Treason" written in 1964 by John A. Stormer. I also quote two lines which I became familiar with from this book which are - "Treason doth never prosper, what's the reason? For if it prosper, none dare call it treason" Sir John Harrington (1561-1612).

In "Why Meditate" I mention two books and one quote from one of the books.

Following the poem, on the same page, I mention:

The above mentioned books are "Finding the Quiet Mind"
by Robert Ellwood. Published by Quest.
"How to Meditate" by Lawrence Le Shan Published by Bantam.

In "Stand Tough" I quote the golden rule: "Do unto others, as you would have others do unto you"

In "The Promised Land" I use the lines "There's money for nothing, chicks for free." This references a Song by the band Dire Straits – "Money for Nothing" - Lyrics by Mark Knopfler.

In "Twilight Zone" the name was inspired by the older, long running TV series "The Twilight Zone" – created by Rod Serling.

This is a self-publishing project and I don't have experience in the field. I don't believe that any of what I have mentioned above, would be considered a copyright infringement anyway, however, as I said above, in an abundance of caution, I thought I'd include the above information.

About the author

I grew up in Cincinnati, Ohio, living in three different neighborhoods and attending three separate school districts – Hyde Park, Madeira and Clifton, respectively. I enlisted in the Navy in 1977 at age 23 as an aviation maintenance administration man.. I did my first tour in an F-14 aircraft squadron at NAS Miramar in San Diego, CA. Then I got out and came back to Cincinnati and stayed in the Naval Reserve for another year and a half. In mid 1982 I went back onto active duty in the Navy at NAS Whidbey Island in Washington State where I did two tours in aircraft squadrons (A-6E and EA-6B). My last tour in the Navy was as ship's company on the USS Nimitz, ported in Bremerton, WA. I separated from the Navy in Oct 1992. In 1993 I basically took a year off work and it was during this time that most of the material in this book was written. In 1994 and early 1995 I attended school at Olympic College in Bremerton Washington. Following this I stayed in Bremerton till late 1998 then returned to Cincinnati, where I currently live. Aside from the Navy, I've held various employment positions over the years, but none of them career oriented.